A New True Book

GIANT PANDAS

By Ovid K. Wong, Ph. D.

CHILDRENS PRESS ®

CHICAGO

Giant pandas are
slow-moving animals.

PHOTO CREDITS
Image Finders:
© R. Flanagan, 2, 14, 25

World Wildlife Fund International: 45 (left)
© Timm Rautert, 7 (left), 10, 19, 38 (left)
© A. Taylor, 21
© Peter Jackson, 24 (left)
© George B. Schaller, 18, 26, 27, 28, 30 (left), 37
(right & left), 39, 45 (right)
© Kojo Tanaka, 4, 30 (right), 43, 44
© Nancy Nash, 41
© Kay Schaller, 38 (right)
© Chris Elliott, 35

H. Armstrong Roberts:
© W. Wittman & H. Miller, Cover, 24 (right)
© Morton D. Spector, 32

The Photo Source: 13

© Lynn Stone: 7 (right)

Tom Stack & Associates:
© Robert C. Simpson, 8
© Tom Stack, 17 (left)
© Brian Parker, 17 (right)

© Jerome Wyckoff, 23

Cover: Giant panda in Toronto zoo

This book is dedicated to my wife — Ada

Library of Congress Cataloging-in-Publication Data

Wong, Ovid K.
  Giant pandas.

  Includes index.
  Summary: Describes the physical characteristics,
habitat, behavior, and endangered situation of China's
national animal treasure.
  1. Giant panda—Juvenile literature. [1. Giant panda.
2. Pandas. 3. Rare animals] I. Title.
QL737.C214W66 1987   599.74'443   87-10717
ISBN 0-516-01241-X

Childrens Press®, Chicago
Copyright ©1987 by Regensteiner Publishing Enterprises, Inc.
All rights reserved. Published simultaneously in Canada.
Printed in the United States of America.
  2 3 4 5 6 7 8 9 10 R 96 95 94 93 92 91 90 89 88

TABLE OF CONTENTS

WHAT IS
THE GIANT PANDA?

The giant panda has a white round face, black eye patches, and black ears. It has a black collar, a white body, a short white tail, and black feet. Its thick fur, measuring two or more inches in places, keeps it warm in winter.

The panda's black and white coat gives it color camouflage. In its shady forest homeland the panda is almost invisible to the hunter at a distance of thirty yards.

Pandas are about five or six feet in length. They can weigh 165 to 300 pounds.

For centuries the Chinese called the panda *beishung*, the white bear. This name is misleading because the panda is not a bear. Like the bear, the giant panda has strong

The skull and digestive system
of the giant panda are similar
to a racoon (right).

teeth and jaw muscles. But
it also has the skull and
digestive system similar
to a raccoon.

For a long time the
classification was
confusing. Did the panda
belong in the bear family?

7

Did it belong in the raccoon family? Finally experts agreed that the giant panda should have its own classification— Ailuropoda melanoleuca.

The giant panda is special.

WHAT IS THE HISTORY OF THE GIANT PANDA?

Fossils of the giant panda have been found that are over four million (4,000,000) years old. According to these fossil records, the early panda was different. Its teeth were longer and stronger suggesting that the giant panda once was a meat

Bamboo leftovers from a panda's meal

eater. Today it eats a variety of foods, especially bamboo plants.

The giant panda was not known to the western world until 1869. It was first discovered by a French missionary naturalist named Abbe

Armand David. In his letter to the Museum of Natural History in Paris, he wrote, "I see a fine skin of the famous white and black bear which appears to be fairly large. It is a very remarkable species...it must constitute an interesting novelty for science."

In 1936, Ruth Harkness, an American, brought a baby panda from China to the United States. The panda was given the name Su-Lin (meaning something very cute). Su-Lin was exhibited in cities, such as San Francisco, St. Louis, and Washington, D.C. The American people were crazy about Su-Lin.

In 1941, the Chinese government gave two giant pandas to the American people. The gift was given to thank the United States for their help. The Chinese delegate said: "...We hope

Panda in the
Peking Zoo

that their (pandas') cute
antics will bring as much
joy to the American
children as American
friendship has brought to
our Chinese people."

Qing Qing and Quan Quan in the Toronto Zoo

In 1972, President Nixon was the first American president to visit The People's Republic of China. To mark this important event gifts were exchanged. Two giant pandas were given to the National Zoo in Washington, D.C. The pandas were named Ling-Ling (meaning the tinkling of small bells) and Hsing-Hsing (meaning a bright star). The United States government gave the Peking Zoo two musk-oxen.

WHERE DO GIANT PANDAS LIVE?

This map shows the area where pandas live.

In the wild, giant pandas can be found only in China. They live in the high mountains near the province of Szechwan. Explorers, hunters, and even natives described the panda's homeland as

Only about 700 pandas still live in the bamboo forests of China.

rugged. Pandas like to hide in the thick forests of evergreen and bamboo trees. The shy pandas rarely leave their forest homes because food is usually plentiful.

The pandas have been forced to move to higher ground and live in nature reserves (opposite page) because farmers have cut down so many bamboo trees in the lowlands.

The homeland of the panda is always cold and wet. Snow stays on the ground from October to May. Other animals also share the land including bears, lynxes, tiger-cats, leopards, monkeys, Asian wild dogs, deer, and many different birds.

WHAT ARE THE
EATING HABITS
OF THE GIANT PANDA?

The giant panda is a
meat eater turned plant
eater. It may eat more
than twenty pounds of
bamboo each day.
Scientists believe that
without bamboo the panda
could not live.

Zhen-Zhen eats bamboo.

The panda is too slow to hunt animals; but it will eat small animals if they are available. The panda may feed at any time of the day or night. However, it eats the most around dawn and in the afternoon.

In zoos pandas eat special meals. Their food may include apples, carrots, cooked sweet potatoes, cooked rice, milk bone, vitamins, and, of course, bamboo.

A zookeeper feeds her panda.

The panda usually sits up to eat. Sometimes it rolls on its back with its feet up in the air while nibbling the young bamboo leaves.

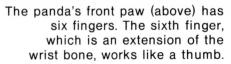

The panda's front paw (above) has six fingers. The sixth finger, which is an extension of the wrist bone, works like a thumb.

The front paws of the giant panda are special because each paw has six fingers. The sixth finger works like a thumb. Using their skillful fingers pandas can peel the outer shell of a plant to reach its juicy center.

HOW DO GIANT PANDAS COMMUNICATE?

Pandas are loners with little social life. When they meet other pandas they make noises. They squeal, chirp, bark, and yip. It is through these sounds that pandas communicate.

25

Scientist examines a panda's scent post in the Wolong Nature Reserve in China.

Pandas do not like strangers in their territory. They mark their territories. Claw markings on trees not only mark their territories, they also help clean and sharpen their nails. Scent markings are

Chinese scientist examines a panda's nesting place.

made by a scent gland under their tail. It has been observed that territorial markings are more frequent during the mating and breeding season when more privacy is desired.

A giant panda surveys the world from its treetop perch.

HOW DO GIANT PANDAS DEFEND THEMSELVES?

In the wild, the pandas have little fear for men. A group of observers reported that they came within a hundred feet of a panda. The animal knew the people were near, but went back to sleep anyway. In other instances pandas climbed trees to escape contact.

Zhen-Zhen visits a field research camp in the Wolong Reserve.

Giant pandas fear dogs because the wild dogs are their natural predators. When cornered by hunting dogs, a panda becomes aggressive. Its claws can inflict nasty wounds. However, unless threatened, a giant panda is normally quiet and docile.

HOW INTELLIGENT ARE GIANT PANDAS?

Intelligence is a very difficult thing to measure. Scientists observe panda behavior to determine how smart the pandas are. Let us examine the following observations.

Ling-Ling lives in the National Zoo in Washington, D.C. She did not like to be shut in the cage when

Pandas are fun to watch.

her larger room was
cleaned. To get what she
wanted, she quickly
learned to sit in the
doorway so the door could
not be closed behind her.

Su-Lin of the Brookfield Zoo in Chicago could not reach some food on a shelf. To get what he wanted he pushed a basket under the shelf and climbed up. As a cub, when his name was called, Su-Lin never failed to turn and respond. The zoo director considered Su-Lin to be very intelligent. His ability to solve problems was compared to the monkeys.

IS THE GIANT PANDA AN ENDANGERED SPECIES?

Fewer than fifteen giant pandas live outside China. They are kept in zoos around the world in cities such as London, Washington, D.C., Madrid, Tokyo, West Berlin, and Mexico City.

In the wild there are fewer than one thousand giant pandas. What causes this small number?

Li-Li guards her cub in the Wolong Research Center.

Basically there are two reasons: slow reproduction and destruction of its food source.

The process of giving birth is slow and multiple births are uncommon. The mother can take care of only one cub every two years. For that reason, if a second cub is born it is usually not taken care of or abandoned.

In China the destruction of the bamboo forest and hunters' traps (set to catch other animals) are the leading causes of panda deaths.

If something is not done either to increase the rate of panda reproduction or to save their bamboo

Scientist examines dead bamboo (left)
in the Wolong Nature Reserve (above).

forests, the giant panda
may soon be extinct.

Recently, reserves and
research centers have
been set up in China. The
reserves protect the
panda's home. The
research center is to find

Radio collars (left) are put on pandas to keep track of their movements.

other ways to save the
animal. For example, field
scientists put radio collars
on the pandas and release
them. These radio signals
tell the scientists where
the pandas are and what
they do.

At the Wolong Research Center scientists
are attempting to improve the breeding of pandas.

Rescue operations are sometimes needed to save the pandas. In 1983, some large bamboo forests near the Wolong Natural Reserve in Szechwan died. The Chinese sent several thousand workers to find starving pandas. The rescued pandas were taken to be fed. Some animals were later sent to zoos. Others were released in forests that had plenty of bamboo.

People from China, the United States, and other countries sent money to save the pandas in 1983. Today the Chinese government and the World Wildlife Fund are continuing this work. They believe, "The giant panda is not only

the precious property of the Chinese people, but also a precious natural heritage of concern to people all over the world."

If an item is rare like gold, its value is high. Because the giant panda is rare, it is priceless.

The giant panda is not for sale to anyone. The pandas that live in most zoos were given as gifts by the Chinese

Chinese children (right) proudly wear panda
stickers (left) distributed by the World Wildlife Fund.

government. To the
Chinese, the giant panda
is a national treasure of
China.

Today, the giant panda
is the symbol of the World
Wildlife Fund's effort to
save all the endangered
animals.

WORDS YOU SHOULD KNOW

aggressive(ah • GRESS • iv) — likely to attack; behave boldly

bamboo(bam • BOO) — a plant of the grass family having tall, hard, but hollow stems

basically(BAY • sick • lee) — having a base; from the beginning

camouflage(KAM • uh • flahj) — colors or designs on an object that make it appear like its background

classification(class • ih • fih • KAY • shun) — a grouping of objects that resemble one another

cornered(KOR • nerd) — forced into a difficult position; trapped

docile(DAH • sil) — gentle; easy to manage

endangered(en • DAYN • jerd) — in danger of dying out

exhibited(ex • IB • it • id) — for public view; shown

extinct(ex • TINKT) — no longer living

fossil(FAWSS • sil) — remains dug out of the earth of plants or animals that lived in past ages

heritage(HAIR • ih • tij) — handed down from one's ancestors

inflict(in • FLIKT) — to cause pain and suffering to another

invisible(in • VIHZ • ih • bil) — hidden; not seen

multiple(MUL • tih • pul) — more than one

naturalist(NATCH • ril • ist) — one learned in natural history; one who believes all religious truths are based in nature

nibbling(NIB • bling) — eating with small, quick bites

observers(ahb • ZER • verz) — persons who are sent to watch and report on animal movements in their natural locations

predator(PREH • di • tir) — an animal that lives by hunting and feeding on other animals

priceless(PRICE • less) — something precious; so valuable its price cannot be estimated

process(PRAH • sess) — all the actions and changes necessary for a result

province(PRAH • vince) — a territory with its own local government within a country

species(SPEE • seez) — a group of closely related animals (or plants) that can mate and produce young

vitamins(VYE • ta • minz) — important minerals necessary for good health

INDEX

About the author

*Ovid Wong earned his B.Sc. degree in biology from the University of Alberta,
Edmonton, Canada, his M.Ed. in curriculum from the University of Washington,
Seattle, and his Ph.D. in science education from the University of Illinois, Urbana-
Champaign. He is currently the science curriculum specialist with school district
#65 in Evanston. Since 1984 he has served as a consultant for the Illinois State
Board of Education and the State Board of Higher Education. He also taught science
at the center for Talent Development, Northwestern University.*
    Dr. Wong's work has appeared on public television and in such journals as
Science Teacher, American Biology Teacher, ISTA Spectrum, The Bilingual Journal
and a number of professional newsletters. Dr. Wong is the author of A Glossary of
Biology. Your Body and How it Works *was published by Childrens Press in 1987.*